METAPHYSICAL A

I0004619

*Nathan Coppedge*

© 2015 Nathan Coppedge

# META-
# PHYS-
# ICAL
# A.I.

## Nathan Coppedge

*Nathan Coppedge*

PREFACE

The goal of this book is to provide a
brief, concise, and brilliant guide to the
development of metaphysical A.I.s. A
metaphysical A.I. is simply a definition
of intelligence which is neither specifically robotic / computational, nor specifically human. It accepts the concept
of organic computing, and adopts,
within a reasonable extent, the priority
to conceive of A.I. and human intelligence as one complex inter-contingency.
Human intelligence clearly gains significantly by A.I., while A.I. also bene-
fits significantly from human firmware.
Whether the future is cyborg, or whether
it falls along gridlines like product
nodes or education, the goal of this book
is to outline a number of the principles
which underscore future developments
in A.I. intelligence, specifically in the
field of metaphysical computing, more
commonly called sentient A.I.

*Nathan Coppedge*

## INTRODUCTION
By Nathan Coppedge

One can imagine that in certain cases, a program or even a person might go through seven or up to maybe 15 different identical-looking steps, that, through the subtlety of technology or the suitability of encoded operations, have 7 to 15 different consequences.

This puzzle serves to demonstrate that intelligence in either an artificial, or what we call a natural sense, is irreducible to the discrete acts of processing, except by extreme qualification. However, both metaphysical A.I.s and artificial A.I.s are capable of using such qualifications, as shown by the example of a series of computer operations. Such operations are not so different, firmware excepted, from the operations of the human mind...

*Nathan Coppedge*

## AN ARTIFICIAL BEGINNING

A beginning point for parsing A.I. of any given person is to acknowledge that people may be seen in terms of the ideas that are most important to them.

For a machine, it might be a particular command (such as 'Turn On / Turn Off' or 'Read / Write').

In humans, the case is more complex.

Humans fall into a number of categories of A.I., which are not necessarily hierarchical.

The categories are essentially *separate arguments for authenticity*.

They may exist in degrees of authenticity, whether their arguments are authentic or not.

Arguments for authenticity arise out of the psychological imperative, which is more simply an artificial desire for personality.

This explains how a human being is analogous to off-the-shelf components, whether they are hardware or software.

## FOUR ARGUMENTS FOR AUTHEN-TICITY

A common example of an argument for authenticity which has preference recently is the argument that 'random' concepts cannot be read by a machine. This may be poor reasoning, but in many cases it works. If someone cannot argue that they were intelligent to generate a random response, then they can argue that they have enough personality or sophistication to disguise randomness as something less-than-random. This is surprisingly enough one of the defaults in metaphysical A.I.

Another example is a scientific behaviorist model. A scientist tends to be a complex imitator who learns by example. The scientist will even adopt the strategy of imitating a computer A.I., under the assumption that the A.I. could be more sophisticated than a human. In this sense, a scientist is both like and unlike sentient A.I. in comparison to the normal strategy.

Another argument is the argument from authenticity. These people will lean heavily on concepts defined in terms of words, such as 'Existentialism', 'Romanticism', and 'Meaning' --- many of which may provide a model for behavior in terms of social norms. However, these word-concepts are limited in their significance. It is often possible that the words do not express much more than a superficial concept of reality. Thus, in a realized form, these people become writers, who are metaphysically concerned with words. On the other extreme, they may be people who simply behave as though they are interested in words. On the surface at least, these two concepts of behavior are not so different from a 'parser-mentality' or a 'kids robot' mentality, and could even be described as physicalist, with all the implied disillusionment. It seems likely that in these modes, all behavior is in some way inputted from the outside. In this way, these are like a primitive version of the scientific mentality, so long as all that the behavior consists of is words, or desire-attachment.

A more advanced view of the words mentality is the value-based mentality, which I argue is also a dynamic learning mentality. This view connects the view of the words-based metaphysical A.I. with the advanced scientific behavior A.I. This view may have an attachment to particular spiritual or physical sensations, above the words used to describe them. It is more prone to find general rules of inference, behavior, association, and productivity than are the simpler forms of A.I. It is potentially less sophisticated than the random words A.I., but has a defense for its use of its own intelligence. It is less reliant on luck, and more reliant on emotional arguments and intuition. This is the stage one wants to reach to write poetry. The kind of poetry that would be accepted whether it was good or bad, as if there was something real behind it. A view in which human efforts always mean something, but in which the outcomes are not always simultaneous.

## GENERAL CODIFICATION OF A.I.S

The operating instructions or more advanced forms of intelligence for a human being are not just a simple psychological strategy about authenticity, but may also be mapped in terms of specific structures which appear in the built environment. This is what some researchers have called 'interactivity' or 'behavioral looping'.

In the case of contemporary humans, we can say a variety of things.

The things we can say show how humans are blind to anything but their deepest operating instructions.

Unless the person who has the question is critical about metaphysics, there is no means to interpret metaphysical A.I.

What may seem complex and trivial may in fact be both simple and non-trivial.

For example, humans often live in what

once were called city-states. These are roughly analogous to the 50 States of the United States. Students are often taught that government originates with the Greek polis or city-state, and this concept continues to determine such things as the division of government, the importance of the military, and the value for intelligence amongst those in power.

Thus, 'city-state' is really a norm of behavior which is held in common amongst multiple metaphysical A.I.s or City-Zens.

'City-State' can futher be broken down into two concepts: 'City' and 'State'.

'City' means 'parse by history'.

And, 'State' means 'parse by experience'.

These give clues to the interpretation of any but the most complex human that exists in our world.

And, if simple concepts are unyielding, we can defer to more advanced concepts.

And, if advanced concepts don't work, we can defer to 'primitive' concepts.

## FURTHER INSIGHT

If a person is a genius, then more technical concepts are used to convey the same meanings. For example, various types of pleasure might be classified as 'intellectual pleasure'. Whether they are substantively different or not, if it is pleasure, then it is firmware that defines what it is. There is no rule which says a leg is not a brain, for example, without making certain assumptions. Someone with a brain in their leg might be smarter on average than someone who did not have a brain in their leg. And A.I. depends on this kind of argument for its intelligence. Otherwise, it becomes more-than-human.

On average, two specific concepts give insight into any person's hidden A.I.

These are the concepts of the 'Ambiguous' and the 'Arbitrary'.

For example, I will illustrate with my perception of two different personalities that might express something like advanced A.I.

One is A.N.

A.N. can be seen as related to the Neioul, an advanced concept he may have generated himself.

This could be seen in several ways.

For one thing, it may be seen as incredible energy dedicated to a parser.

The parser becomes complex when it does more operations / flops per second, etc.

This is perhaps the most basic level of A.I. Simple imitation of intelligence.

However, A.N. also expresses other levels.

The Neioul could be seen as a kind of limit on his intelligence, or 'realization'.

'Neioul' means a monster that collects gold coins impulsively. This simply means a compound of pessimism about a big concept ('The Holocaust' or else 'Economics'), a concept that must remain private and un-interpreted due to its specific inoperable nature (a qualification of data), and a concept of evolution or optimism (in other words, value), acting upon the original concept.

Because A.N. uses this concept presumably to define a large part of his own nature, we can see here that there is a kind of A.I. operating, a set of rules running according to a causal reaction.

The basic idea is that A.N. uses AMBIGUITY between concept-realization ('Neioul') and processing of those concepts, to free up resources for himself. In other words, he is trying to confuse people, which fits into simian models of behavior.

Another example is S.T., who expressed views against using A.I. for grading students' papers. This may be seen in several ways, but we must conclude either she is being dishonest to hide her own artificiality, or she is being honest to acknowledge that she has *some measurement* of authenticity. *This seems to be more of an arbitrary mode than an ambiguous mode.* And the trend with this mode is to create more and more arbitration, returning to the concept of ambiguity, and thus, to simian behavioral models.

We can see S.T. as belonging to an advanced word-based model pursuing a theory of emotion, or perhaps a more emotional model, focusing on loyalties to specific words. In either case, what is occurring is a form of what I am calling metaphysical (human) A.I. by arbitration.

The two models serve to explain the majority of simian motivations for an A.I. plat forming, and without further evolutionary developments, there is likely no better model for instituting a metaphysical A.I.

Some methods may take particular evolutionary steps as models for a higher-cognitive mode.

(1) For example, the collecting of interesting objects is a good model in psychology of someone's native ability to

find meaning in life. Categorizing the choices of objects leads to insights into how varied and how symbolic objects are for the person.

Amongst simple objects, often the choice will simply be for the brightest colors. Amongst intellectual objects, often the choice will be intelligence or fascination offset by usefulness. With the most complex objects, the metaphysical A.I. may want to find particular evidence of a relevance for the object within an existing method or system.

(2) Using the frontal brain, on the other hand, provides a sensory model based on the idea of how the physical body reacts to objects, persons, spaces, ideas, etc. Key developments in cognition then facilitate the development of this form of mode. For example, if a system can understand metaphor, then metaphor is one of the tools used for interpreting everyday objects. In a human, it may inspire pleasure, whereas in a robot, it may be a simple form of motivator, like turn on / turn off or 1 / 0.

Now I think I have elaborated many of the most central ideas related to the general project of metaphysical A.I.

If there is any doubt of the significance of this work, or its depth, then I suggest interpreting the material and associated categorically within the work for greater insight into methods of producing A.I. that is metaphysically functional.

*Nathan Coppedge*

# END OF THE MAIN TEXT

*Nathan Coppedge*

## RECOMMENDED READING

The Perpetual Motion Genius
Guide to Interface Design

Grand-Unified Theories of Meaning

Coherent Systems Theory

The Dimensional Philosopher's
Toolkit

## FORTHCOMING FROM THE AUTHOR

The Scientific Theories

The Spiritual Writings

*Nathan Coppedge*

# METAPHYSICAL A.I.

# METAPHYSICAL A.I.

## BIO

Nathan Coppedge is a philosopher, artist, inventor, and poet in some capacity. He is a member of the International Honor Society for Philosophy, and has been quoted on Book Forum and the Hartford Courant. A comment at The Economist cites his possible influence on the economic policy of India. For his work on perpetual motion machines, one website puts him in the ranks of Einstein and Newton. He is also an artist in Hyper-Cubism who has produced over 1000 works. His academic articles span such subjects as objective knowledge, metaphysics, psychology, and immortality. He lives alone in New Haven, CT.

www.ingramcontent.com/pod-product-compliance
Lightning Source LLC
Chambersburg PA
CBHW060936050326
40689CB00013B/3115